Dedication

This book is dedicated to my cousin, Judie Arceneaux. You have helped me to stand. You've helped to re-energize my faith. You were like a dance of love and God's blessings. What a joy it is to be your cousin!

I thank my God every time I remember you.

Philippians 1:3

Dare To Dance: Tapping Into Spiritual Renewal

Spiritual Growth in Everyday Life

To Andrew

Giving thanks for your compassion, understanding and understanding, I say "Thank you."

[signature]

Dare To Dance: Tapping Into Spiritual Renewal

Spiritual Growth in Everyday Life

M. MARVA ALLISON

authorHOUSE®

AuthorHouse™ LLC
1663 Liberty Drive
Bloomington, IN 47403
www.authorhouse.com
Phone: 1-800-839-8640

Published by AuthorHouse 11/18/2013

ISBN: 978-1-4918-2525-9 (sc)
ISBN: 978-1-4918-2524-2 (hc)
ISBN: 978-1-4918-2523-5 (e)

Library of Congress Control Number: 2013918095

Bible references in this book are from the New Revised Standard Version unless otherwise indicated.

All Scriptures unless otherwise noted, are taken from the King James Version of the Bible.

Contents

Preface

This book, of easy reading, yet hard hitting spiritual information, is designed to transform your spiritual journey. Whatever challenges you may be facing, at this moment, in this season and at this time, can be addressed through prayers, meditation and affirmations.

Out of a deep desire to become healed emotionally, physically and spiritually, the vision for this book was born. In search of the right words and materials needed to develop my spiritual renewal,everything available was read,studied and gobbled. This included the Bible, inspirational books, magazines, meditation books, gospel and spiritual music, television ministries, attending bible classes, retreats as well daily and Sunday mass journaling and notetaking.

By doing these things, I became more aware of steps needed to be more fully aware of spiritual tools that are useable to develop lasting spiritual growth. "Do whatever it takes to bring life to its fullest" are words that might seem overwhelming or frightening but worked as a mantra for me. Putting "legs on my faith" and "planting seeds of faith" gave me a release to give God my best. Using spiritual mind treatments, aligning affirmations, meditating, inspirational readings as well as music and songs, I began to take more time in an attempt to get a better understanding and assessment of my "spiritual" belief and life.

Do you take the time to pray, meditate or practice affirmations? Today, most everyone is busy or on the move.; at home or out in the work force. And yet with so much "output" and some "input", quick as well as easy engaging spiritual "refills" are needed to get that renewed and energized spirit. In Ephesians 5:18, it states, "Be filled with the Spirit". Time and time again, the Bible stresses the power of prayer. The scriptures indicate that problems and afflictions are a "normal" part of life which has a need for "spiritual" growth. One of the ways some people use to increase "spiritual" transformation is through praying.

Take an honest assessment of your spiritual life and decide what works for you. Allow your imagination to "see" and "hear" God's presence in your life. With each step explore the Scriptures and come to terms with your spiritual self. You are invited to pray and use whatever steps, not just once, but many times to help you positively dig deeper into a relationship and friendship with God. Daily set aside time to "dance", expressing devotion to God. "David danced before the Lord with all his might". (2 Samuel 6:14)

Discovering through the years that learning to pray offered me an experience that was most rewarding. It has influenced my desire to learn more about types of prayers, reasons for praying as well as how to pray. In order to develop a greater intimacy with Christ, I have found reading the Bible, stop and pray about what you have read then He will direct your steps. Evelyn Christenson stated "God is the only author who is always present with us when we read."

Through this book, readers, I hope that you can discover your incredible potential for a deeper walk with God as you enjoy the change of relationship that you will develop as you dance with the most "grace-ful partner of all, Jesus Christ."

"For in Him we live and move and have our being." (Act 17:28)

Introduction

Daily, for an hour, I begin my day in "gratitude" expressing my love for God. I have found by doing this, my day gets off to a better start. Combining daily inspirational reading from "Science of the Mind", "Daily Word", "The Upper Room", "The Word" and selected Scriptures for the Day, I channel my prayers and faith into a physical form of worship. The peace, joy and hope that I find doing these exercises release my energy. Other times, overcome with grief for Christ's sacrifice, I am so carried away that the hour flies by without my noticing.

Finding that praying is an amazing way to worship God, and to express your love for Him is a great experience. Think about it: From ancient time use of prayers, worship, celebration even songs gave meaning and feelings to praise "our creator". When David decided to dance before the Lord, I know exactly how he felt. He was simply pouring out his love and gratitude to God. Praying, with my whole heart and soul is breath taking. All kinds of praying can be used in worship as an outpouring of love for God; that's all that matters. Praying moves, inspires and gives a meanful way to express how we feel. Sometimes, when my heart is too full to form words, I put on music and move. My heart energizes my muscles, my eyes are closed and my heart is set on the Lord. I am a prayer "in motion". Lifting my hands or looking up toward heaven, kneeling in sorrow incorporated with my prayers make my interaction with God more substantial in good times and bad. My prayers become a dance before God. Bring to the Lord your joys and sorrows. Choose a **Psalm** that expresses your feelings. (Look for one set to music or gospel CD) and "pray in motion". In Ecclesiastes 3:2, it states, "there is a time … or crying and laughing, weeping and dancing." Through insights, God teaches lessons for living so that we can stay the course. Somethings are easier said without words. During spiritual development, ask God to give "insight" so that you can do what He is telling you. Read Psalm 119:23; pray for the courage to enter into awkward conversations with others or topics that are considered off limits i.e. sex, sexuality etc. Instead of searching the internet for answers, pray for courage to enter into awkward conversations with others. There are bold ways to change the world and speak about faith; like John's dreams and actions in "Revelation" and quite ways like a shadow healing the sick. Building faith and improving spiritual growth includes coming to terms with our own circumstances, wounds and realities as you explore the Scriptures, prayers, meditation, affirmations, songs and music to explain the many topics that might need explanations. Galatians 5:22-23 can be used as a guide on conversations addressing patience, joy, kindness, love, and self-control.

In 2 Thessalonians 1:3 it states "your faith is growing more and more, act on it; talk honestly about what is going on in your life and what you believe God has to say and see how your faith grows." Whenever you feel challenges, by "outer turmoil", turn inside and chose your thoughts. Learning that when you hold close to your faith, hope replaces doubt and you become more energized has helped to overcome obstacles and discouragements. Make the dancing continue; connect praying, hymns, liturgical dances that can "usher" you into the presence of

God. Combining prayer, meditation, affirmations and movement will set you free for an honest, intimate encounter with the One who leads you in the "dance of life".

Giving "birth" to a new consciousness and spiritual awareness, help to see beyond the world of "effect". Think with God "all things are possible". In the past, when I could not see a clear path, I held on to faith, hope and replace doubt with possibilities. Hearing the words "you have breast cancer" was enough to challenge my faith. Focusing on this obstacle helped me to rethink my relationship with God. Allowing God's grace and love to guide me through this difficult period, helped me to begin a process of spiritual growth that led me to a deeper faith, spiritual growth, friendship and relationship with God.

Learning that life is full of blessings, mysterious beyond expectations and understanding is much like dancing; God leads and you follow. As with dancing, a partner is learning how to listen, to feel the rhythm and paying attention to the interaction. Sometimes you are not sure of how you have changed but God does dance with you . . . dance of love.

One

First Thing First

Dare to Dance: Tapping into the Spirit . . . is not a prayer book.

Its style enables you to apply the truth of God's words to your spiritual growth and development, your prayer life and your life in general. The information is based directly from Scriptures. This book has a variety of uses. One of the most important uses is to help make a major breakthrough in your spiritual growth and approach to prayers as you confront those issues on the power and authority of the Word of God. This is a fantastic tool for personal Bible study and a personal reference book that will help you to grow in faith, trust God more fully and a marvelous means for memorizing the Word of God.

This is a "life-style" book that shows you how to cultivate and continue to find full freedom and deliverance in God. It will help you experience faith, joy, hope and life changing peace you have acquired as a result of reading Dare to Dance: Tapping Into the Spirit . . . . This book is multifaceted. It is a result of much reading and "intense" inspiration by the Holy Spirit. Having read much, lived much, suffered much and matured, "letting go and letting God" I have overcome many obstacles. Holding on to my faith, even when my path was not clear, I knew in my heart that all things would work out for my good. Renewing, refocusing and establishing my thinking and my activities, I gave thanks to God for working in me and through me.

Think about how amazing it is to have an opportunity to personally "commune" with

God. Making contact with God through prayers, meditation, reading the Bible and/or making personal affirmation is simply "fellowshipping" with God. It is talking to Him as well as listening to Him. It is setting aside time from the distractions and demands of life and taking the time to develop as well as strengthen your commitment to put things first and make a daily connection with God.

If you want to see what God can do, it is necessary to "build" your schedule around Him. You cannot be satisfied to work Him into your schedule when it is convenient. You must seek God in prayer and the Word every day, whether things are hard or easy, in good times and in bad. In James 4:8, He gave His word. In Hebrew 10:22, it says, "Let us draw near with a true heart in full assurance of faith . . ."

When you call on God, you will never be answered by "voice mail".

The moment you turn to Him, He will be there for you. That is why it is important to put first things first. Daily contact with God is vital to your spiritual experience. In a moment, just one word from God can change your whole situation. Your victory is won first in the heart then in circumstances. Jesus is your "life force."

Cultivating a consistent spiritual practice reinforces your ability to bring the realization of God in your life. "Keeping it real" means to make the presence of God the most important aspect of your daily life. Today, make a plan to put God first in your life. As you commit, to living your life, using spiritual tools, you will notice more positive things will happen. This will happen because you bring the realization that God is in charge.

Allowing God's plan will aid in removal of frustration, pain and challenges you encounter in life's lessons.

First, by seeing God's perspective and praying for God's power to let go and letting Him be in charge will lead to more joy and less frustration. Stop trying to carry it all and allow God to take charge. "Hold fast to the Lord your God, as you have done to this day". (Josh. 23:8)

There is an old adage that states "if your plan is not God's plan, it is just a joke." Do not allow the enormity of the problem to stop you from taking the first step. Assert your freedom, step by step, thought by thought, take a new look at yourself, a new look at your life and press on. Your anchor in the Rock is unmovable; Jesus Christ.

Until you make a commitment, nothing happens in your life.

Infuse your mind with your vision. Commit to see your blessings and feel gratified. You are one with God who fashioned the human soul, made life and made a wonderful spiritual connection.

God asks us to "take the first step" because it enhances the growth of faith. Allow God's presence to settle into your bones and allow your soul, "the freedom to sing, dance, praise and love". Celebrate with grace and invoke God's love.

Two

Keeping It Real

Unity co-founder Myrtle Fillmore reminded us that a spiritual power is always at work in our lives, guiding and blessings us whether we are aware of it or not. Just as we cannot see the wing but see the evidence of its power as leaves flutter on trees or hear its roar, as you bring the realization of the Spirit to all that you do, you begin to live from a place of knowing that "all 's well".

Keeping it real means to realize that God is in your life. It means to make the presence of God the most important aspect of your daily life. Giving thanks for the rich variety of life on earth, treasured memories and expressions of love, helped to infuse life with God's words help to shape your consciousness and heart to realize that all things are possible "Be transformed by the renewing of your mind" (Romans 12:2)Thus your minds are unveiled to the wisdom as well as inspiration of God. Turning within for spiritual wisdom and serenity, I experience the peace that "passes all understanding."

(see Phil 4:7)

No one could have told me that ten years later, I would be around to tell my story. Now instead of questioning God, displaying actions of disbelief, I have learned that "joy returns after suffering."

This might sound crazy but as many have said "cancer was the best thing that could have happened to me." It gave me an opportunity to enter into a relationship with God that was more intimate. It allowed.me to experience and seek more of God in my life.

My prayers were not answered in the way or time I had envisioned but I learned to trust that God was in charge and the best was yet to come. In Ecclesiastes 3:1, it states "for everything there is a season, and a time for every matter under heaven", my season was evident. To move beyond my fear, I remembered the truth of my existence. Behind the mask, the true me came out.

At first, the fact that I had been diagnosis with breast cancer I was afraid, discouraged and in doubt. My belief as well as faith was challenged. Finding myself questioning God, I realized that no one had the answer to my pain. Embarking upon a desperate search to understand what

God had to say about my health challenge, I gradually sought the "theological" perspective behind suffering.

Wrestling with the question of "God"; why God, where is God? and finally looking to God's words for answers, I realized that He had given me the necessary spiritual tools, stamina and the ability to face the realities of breast cancer. As Job declared "man was born for trouble." The road to recovery would be a long one. Although, I had survived the surgery, breast reconstruction, chemotherapy, the aches and pains as well as mental stress, there were still challenges. I had decided that I was willing to "fight in faith."

Learning to adapt this new lifestyle, praying to align my body, pains and thoughts with God's will and scriptures, I read that it is not His will that I should suffer or remain ill. Standing firm on Is. 54:7, proclaiming "that no weapon formed against us shall prosper", I adjusted to the regiments of doctor's visit, blood work, special diet and thirty six treatments of radiation. Constantly reminded that God said, "Your life on earth is not about you. It's about me" So despite my circumstances, I have learned to praise God, developed a friendship and relationship with Him. For everything in my life, I have learned to praise God. Fighting the good fight in faith is described in my book ***It's Time To Sing My Song: Overcoming Circumstances with Faith.*** Paul Dean Jackson, of Glenside said it best, "With Spirit, anything is possible; anything begins anew". In gratitude, daily I give thanks to God for being alive and counted as a cancer survivor. Looking back, now I better understand how faith and prayers have been and will continue to be important parts of my recovery and survival.

Making a commitment to take one step at a time to be a healthier and happier me, "I will give thanks to the Lord with my whole heart; I will tell of all your wonderful deeds". __ Psalm 9:1 it's a spiritual voyage opened to guidance.

Continuing to count on God, turning to Him in prayer, praising Him by clapping, singing and stepping, I continue to dance in the Spirit. Again, if anyone had told me ten years ago that I would be a breast cancer survivor, despite the unexpected changes to my carefully laid out plans; retirement, traveling etc. that lead to taking a stance in the Word of God did not seem real. Now I am enjoying retirement while sharing and doing God's will. He has promised to meet every need (Matt. 6:36) My life is different but not defeated. I am not at the mercy of some habits or illness that does not contribute to my well-being. I am a "spiritual being, unfettered and free." Unlimited by former thoughts and feelings, turning to prayer, I feel the reassurance of God's love.

This love strengthens my resolve, bolsters my courage and guides my steps.

I know that God is not finished with me. Fully using the power of the Spirit within me to be free from restraint, I open up to the understanding that I have the power here and now to do all things in Christ. My life is bursting with God's promises. I have often heard the phrase "In all things, we give thanks". I must confess that sometimes I have silently wondered. "Really?" "All things"?

At first I did not get it. The more freedom I experience physically, mentally, emotionally and spiritually was my introduction to gratitude. That is thank you God and let me show what it means to me . . . a commitment to action; to show my family and the world what having faith can do. Faith moved the mountains in my life. (See Matthew 17:20) Refueling my energy and replenishing my "fuel", opened my feelings to higher awareness as the space between musical notes and harmony, so too, does the creative expressions of Spirits. Each day thrive to grow, be flexible, bend with the "winds of changes, step and sway, in the breeze of life". Spiral upward, seeing with fresh eyes is moving as well as awakening to celebrating life that moves your spirit.

Take time to attune and reconnect with your spiritual nature.

Start moving your feet. Take thirty seconds and dance. Praise God. In Nahum it states: The Lord is good . . . he protects those who takes refuge in him, even in a rushing flood.

You must be flexible in your attitude, expectations and views.

By being flexible, you open yourself to growth, progress and gain a new appreciation of life. Therefore, when challenges arrive, you can sway in the "breezes of life" and direct your footsteps to the beat.

Three

On Life's Detours

You are the "light of God". This is the highest ideal that you should keep at the forefront of your mind. As you keep this thought first and foremost in your mind, you will find there is nothing that can keep you from fulfilling your life's dream. Step fully into your life like there is no tomorrow. Do whatever it takes to bring the pure realization of God and be lifted as well as gifted with the fullness of life.

Rise up strong and unafraid. Tangle with what you fear the most.

Grab Jesus's hand, keep your eyes straight ahead and press on.

If it seems that your life is always under construction, with a sign "close for repair", or a "work in progress" trust in the Lord with all your heart and lean not on your own understanding. In all your ways acknowledge him; and He shall direct your path. (Proverb 3:5-6)

Believe me there is no better feeling than spending time with your heavenly father. And you know what He feels the same way about you being with Him. **You can't but I can. With me all things are possible. Now go. Take time and affirm His power.**

Life chocking situations, nagging spirits, sarcastic comments and critical jabs start to take over. Eliminating these will not happen overnight. But with persistent determination, heartfelt determination, prayers and the power of the

Holy Spirit, you will get back on the right path. Ask God to improve your spiritual journey by praising Him and asking for a fresh "infilling" of the Holy Spirit's power in your life. In Hebrew2:1, "We must pay more careful attention, therefore, do what we have heard, so that we do not drift away".

Reflect on how you read the Bible. Grab God's Words and read this masterpiece. He speaks through every "stroke of the writer's pen" into your life.

Despite the difficulties, drawing blanks, becoming confused, or unexpected problems, running this great race of life with the persistence that only God can give is a victory. If you listen closely, you will hear the applause of heaven for each victory. "Cast all your worries upon Him because He cares for you. (1 Peter 5:7)

Casting all of your worries upon the Lord, might look impossible to you but not to the Lord. You can give Him all of your worries. Do not allow big worries and even smaller nagging concerns to sap your strength or rob you of your joy and spiral you into doubt and despair.

Every generation has had its worriers. This is evident by the universal words of scriptures (see Matthew 6:25; Phil 4:6). And even though today's worries maybe justifiable, or seem to be more numerous than in past ages, the biblical injunctions remain and they demand a response.

A *misconception* of "God" is another major cause of worry.

Some Christians are convinced that God does not want them be happy or successful. Other people believe that God has stopped loving them. Once you learn to distinguish between what you can and cannot control, you can decrease your worry. Read how contemporary a two thousand year old statement sounds:

"Therefore do not be anxious for tomorrow; for tomorrow will take care for itself. Each day has enough trouble of its own" (Matt. 6:36)

Live one day at a time. Or as Ziggy says, "Why worry about tomorrow. We may not make it through the day."

Have you forgotten God's great love for you? "Fear not, for I have redeemed you. I have called you by name, you are mine"

(Isaiah 43:1) In your heart, God puts a song in this great race of life and God's message come through loud and clear. The hymn writer wrote, "Take your burdens to the Lord and leave them there." The Scriptures give four reasons why you should bring your worries to God in prayer. (1) Because God already knew my needs and worries (Matt. 6:8, 31), (2) Because God is able to meet your needs and remove your worries (Matt. 6:26, 27-30); (3) Because God wants to provide for you (1 Pet. 5:7); and (4) Because prayers produces results (Phil. 4:6-7)

Many of the Lord's promises lie dormant because no one claims them. Develop the habit of taking God at His Word. You will spend less time worrying. In Psalm 86:11, there is a godly guideline just waiting to be discovered; "Teach me your ways, O Lord, and I will walk in your truth." All day God speaks to us through other people, circumstances, and pain. "Let us fix our eyes on Jesus, the author and perfecter of our faith (Hebrew 12:2) Amazing grace, how sweet the sound. Janelle Spooner of *Guidepost said* "prayer is a wonderful thing. It calms us. It heals us. It gives us strength to face the unknown. God reveals the power of who He is and His purpose in your life.

Our heavenly father is both willing and able to answer when you call on him. What request will you bring before your heavenly father?

What do you battle? Deadlines? Discouragements? Chronic pains?

A fear or worry of any kind? Co-workers? Add a list of your own battles. Remember that you receive the power you need to stand victorious in your daily battles.

Scott Peck became famous for the opening sentence of his book, *The Road Less Traveled*: "Life is difficult". So how do you find the courage to keep on praying? Pray affirmatively and become aware that you "stand in the Truth of your being". Witness the power of prayer in your life! In Exodus 33:14, it states "My presence will go with you, and I will give you rest." Become refresh and ready to move forward. Tap, slide, bounce and grow in the spirit of joy.

Four

Connecting to Faith

How can you connect the Spirit of God's ministry in your life?

You connect to your power supply by faith. Just as you personally invite Him into your life (an act of faith, see John 5:14, 15 and Eph. 5:18) you can invite the Holy Spirit to control your life.

As I searched the Scriptures, going humbly to God and meekly, admitting that I needed His instructions, I frequently prayed.

A statement that Steve Harvey made, referring to his grandmother brought it home to me. Steve Harvey said that his grandmother told him to always "pray" and pray some more. Reverend

Ossie Smith, Jr., pastor of Covenant Church, in South Holland, IL and one of the greatest Bible instructor stated that "we should always praise Him. Get up praising Him. Praise Him all the time."

My spiritual barometer for years has been *1 John 1:4* "these things { are written} that your joy may be full." Spending time in the Scriptures taught me that the Bible has an answer for every situation.

It has proven to me that the Bible truly is a *living Book.* "For the Word of God is living and active, "Hebrew 4:12 tell us. It has answers in the "midst of our knowledge explosion today—_or tomorrow_".

These months of searching Scriptures had been a private experience in my life, unplanned, but rewarding. Praying silently and trying to put things together, I decided to attend a week-end Women retreat, with a group of Women, from my home church, St. Ailbe, in Chicago, Illinois. This was a first for me; Emmaus retreat.

On Friday evening, we had a meet and greet and got our materials, sharing a prayer and dinner, we were off to prepared for Saturday's activities. It was a fast paced and moving weekend. One of the final activities was to pair-off with a seasoned member of the retreat team for "one on one" conversation. Following that activity, we were to write a letter to that person detailing how this experience had changed our lives. Then, seal the letter and turn it into the team leader for distribution at the end of the retreat. This was a very moving experience. God opened the door and made me feel comfortable to share as well as pray with my new found "sisters in faith".

Holding hands and singing "Blest be the Tie that Binds" with tears flowing, on to mass we went. This was one of the most moving experiences of my church life. It nourished our relationship with Him so that we could continue to grow in faith and draw us into a closer relationship with Him. Our Savior, Jesus, promises in Matthew 10:22, "The one who stands firm to the end will be saved." He will bring us through the toughest trials. My new found "faith-filled friends" helped me to focus on His power, instead of our feelings. Thank you God for new friends and learning about faith and trust.

A pattern emerged. We started staying alert to each other's needs. We learned to lean more heavily on the Holy Spirit and to take our needs to the Father. Around the clock prayer chains were developed. A Christian book club was developed. Street corner ministries were developed. The miracle of love, life and faith brought faith down from the clouds and into day-to-day situations. We did learn that life is a process of growth. It just does not happen. Right now we have an opportunity to say "yes!" to life, to be alive and aware of the wondrous of energy of God in my life. Grateful for the fullness of my life and the opportunity to live it well is very precious.

God chose me! Focused on God. Your path will be really okay.

Life is full of mysteries. Some of them are too perplexing. Thomas Moore said "Aging forces us to decide what is important in life."

Whether you chose to waltz or dance around to the tune of Kirk Franklin, God does not care as long as you praise Him. The moments that bind you to God are most powerful. Hallelujah! Oh, come on. Give it a try. May the God who gives endurance and encouragement give you spirit of unity among yourselves as you follow Christ Jesus. (Romans 15:5)

Step forward in confidence. Receive new insights into the situations of your life. Allow the pure uplifting joy of prayer help to keep you energized. When prayers seem to go unanswered, you can say for one thing that God did not turn away. Jesus is Emmanuel, which means "God is with us." E. Stanley Jones said it this way: "Jesus puts a face on God." And you find courage to keep on praying. By the power of praying, discover your spiritual strength and regrow your spirit naturally. Be bold! Believe! Explore!

Literally, stop and pray. Stay centered on an opportunity to praise Him. God promises to guide you on the right path.

Five

Spiritual Market

Maybe I am just old fashioned. *I know that things have to change.* In today's church, what kinds of events make us rise to our feet? Is there such a thing as a "new life" in Christ? One of questions should be are we tuned in to God? Another question is are we committed to His good news as we work to serve, share His love and keep His commandants? Are we spoke persons for God?

We are ordinary people that the Lord has called to do His "extraordinary" work. We are called to tell the good news and the "prophetic voices" the world needs to hear.

"Life is not about waiting for the storm to pass . . . it's about learning to dance in the rain." Moving alertly and reflectively, we do not have to be a theologian or a Bible scholar to understand that God is more than enough to meet our needs and challenges. How often do we miss opportunities to follow God's leading because of being afraid or unsure of the consequences? In John 14:6, Jesus said I am the way and the truth and life."

Engaging with God and His Word is about as good as it gets. Be reminded of Ephesians 3:20, which assured that God was able to do all things exceedingly above all that we ask of thought.

Lynette Holloway stated that Bishop T. D. Jakes, one of America's most influential spiritual leaders and those like him have re-packaged the maxim for the message to resonate today. In his books, Bishop Jakes maps out a spiritual journey, guided by scriptures for people looking for a new lease on life, whether they are just starting out, starting over or just wanting to move to another level.

Other authors in this spiritual book "burgeoning" market include books by Evelyn Christenson, Joyce Myers, Diane Graham and Julie Norris, Noel Jones, Joel Osteen, Tony Evans, Rick Hamlin, Bishop E. Bernard Jordon, Tim LaHaye, Pope Benedict XVI, Sharif Abdullah Deepak Chopra, Lisa Nichos and Michael Bernard Beck, Rhonda Byrne. Susan Taylor, Wayne Dyer and Dr. Norman Vincent Peale.

The publishing industry sees the spiritual books as an answer to "wavering" book sales. Desire Sanders, president of Afrocentric Bookstore, on the South side, in Chicago, Illinois said "people are reading more spiritual books as well as inspirational books."

Tony Rose, publisher and chief executive officer of the African American owned Amber Communication Group, in Phoenix, Arizona, which publishes inspirational books, agrees with Sanders.

"You are talking about a genre that is positive," he said. These books do not replace the **Bible.** Also, these books seem to open the door to infinite supply, ever-renewing life and spiritual fulfillment.

In John 15:7, "If you abide in me, and in my words abide in you, ask for whatever you wish, and it will be done for you." Jesus showed that enhancing your understanding and following His guidance will aid in the development of unquestioning faith.

The music world has enjoyed the growth of gospel music and Inspirational songs sale. According to Emillo, music "transports me to a place where there is no worries, no sadness". Gloria Estefan stated that she has "seen the healing "power of music in the lives of others too." Music heals and it can be a way of crying. Gospel and inspirational music addresses love, faith, family as well as all emotions connected to the human experience. When struggling with fear, worries, self-doubt and day to day existence, some songs can stretch you and help you to grow in the spirit. Just think of Kirk Franklin's rendition of "Smile". Sing it over and over and it will become second nature to you. Then let the words go and trust God. Connect the dots. You could experience an "Eureka Moment"; equivalent to "I've got it"! Life is full of choices and full of decisions.

Nothing can raise your spirits like a great song. Song of Praise and Joy, prayers and the true love of God can keep God's Words in your heart. Every once in a while, a song is written that is divinely inspired that have become classics. Others have a contemporary spin to spiritual songs that you have enjoyed all your life. Your favorite songs are performed by various singers, church leaders from churches around the country. Their talents and faith are the perfect combination for bringing God's peace and love into your life.

You will find these praise songs to be uplifting and soul stirring; ideal for everyday inspiration. "Sing the praises of the Lord, you His faithful people; praise His holy name". (Psalm 30:4) Songs can be broken down into: *Songs of Praise, Songs of Faith, Songs of Prayers and Songs of Jesus.* Titles such as "Amazing Grace", "O, Magnify the Lord",

"Rock of Ages," "Come Holy Spirit"," He is Able", Come Holy Ghost" are a few spirit lifting songs that you will love to listen to as you relax, drive, exercise or in the presence of God. Praise songs that make you feel closer to God like "We Fall Down" "Father, I Adore You" are songs created to soothe, celebrate and offer hope. Also, songs of remembrance and hope such as "Precious Lord, Take My Hand", "The Lord's Prayer", "Ava Maria", "Peace in the Valley" are just a few that come to mind. This spirit-filled songs can offer moments of peace and hope. These songs satisfied, enlighten and inspire its listeners. They are divinely inspired by deep and abiding faith. Think about it! Add your own favorite songs.

Gospel music sales, in recent years have exploded. Gospel music has grown on mainstream radio format nationally. "Christians are supporting gospel music and record sales" said Cheryl Jackson, Program Director of Washington, D.C's Stellar Award. The rapid growth of technology has had a direct impact. People can now down load music to their computers, cell phones, I Pods, tablets and other electronic equipment. Many big name artists are on television channels such as TBN, BET, CBN and other gospel TV outlets. Some regional channels carry gospel music, movies as well as videos.

Despite the inventions, interventions, technology, there is a constant process of renewal. "A super intelligence exists in each of us which is infinitely smarter and possesses of technical know-how far beyond our present understanding," explained the renowned biologist Lewis Thomas. Make you stop and think "where are my priorities?"

The publishing industry sees spiritual book "niche" as an answer to wanning sales". Indeed, interest in spiritual books comes at a time when the nation is experiencing economic uncertainty, political unrest and war in Afghanistan. Indeed reading spiritual books and listening to inspirational and gospel music help to drive home the message of the spiritual word. Again, these books will not replace the Bible, but sales of hymnals, and pray books will allow you to experience God not only on Sunday but anywhere and anytime.

Looking beyond and allowing God to expose the treasurers just waiting to be discovered; "At just, the right time we will reap a Harvest of blessings if we don't give up" (Galatians 6:9)*The Science of Mind* teaches God is forever doing new things and when we conceive new ideas, it is an Act of the Divine . . . How exciting it is!

What's "trending" in your world? For what are you thirsty? You are given the gift of exploring with the expectation that you will do your best to learn what that entails and accept the responsibility to live in God's friendship. Remember the old song "Que Sera, Sera"? Disguised that "whatever will be, will be" was found to be clever but not always true. Abraham Lincoln said "Be sure to put your feet in the right place, then stand firm." Give yourself permission to experience the "Divine" flow.

Plug into God. Move beyond the barriers. Through reading, songs, spiritual technology, inspiring words give steps to your inner most journey back to the light and care of God.

Six

Reflecting on Praying

One of the most often question asked is "what's the best way to pray?" Actually, according to Albert Haase, O.F.M., the best way to pray "is the way that works best for you." Also, he suggests that you try different techniques and find one that suits you. The most important thing is that your prayers are supposed to make you "prayful". Prayers should make us "attentive to the presence of God in the here and now."

Some people pray for a "road to Damascus experience" like Paul that will change their lives forever. "Unfortunately, that prayer might continue to go unanswered. Most people are like the disciples on the road to Emmaus . . . struggling with blindness and discouragements" did not see Jesus as He walked with them. In 1Peter 5:7 it states "Casting all your cares upon Him for He careth for for you." This statement might aid in your believing as well as trusting in God's unwavering love.

The journey to knowing God is a daily one. As you keep your mind opened to inspiration and guidance, your faith in God will increase and so will faith in yourself. The Spirit will reveal to you what you must do to grow and succeed; "Have faith in God". (-Mark 11:22)

Whenever going to work, to church, to school, doing routine task, or having a new experience fulfillment should be done in prayer.

Even when you are not making major decisions, make a commitment to keep God in the plan.

"Commit your ways to the Lord; trust in Him and He will act"—Psalm 37:5. Move forward with confidence. Praying should make you "attentive to the presence of God in the here and now."

Prayer has the power to transform any condition. In prayer, people release themselves and lives to God. In the strictest sense, prayer is a humble religious petition of man to God to seek divine benevolence and benefits he needs for life, both temporal and eternal. It is a conversation with God, either by accepted prayer form or from the heart. Asking for spiritual, material goods, for health, money success, help for others, difficult situations, healing is a form of praying. Unity teaches, to turn pray fully inside and affirm that God is the giver of life and wholeness. When you are praying for healing for others or yourself, keep your attention centered on the dynamic, invigorating life of God that dwells in your body. Do not be tempted to talk of illness, suffering or negative symptoms. Turn prayerfully and affirm that God is the giver of life and wholeness. "I am, the Lord who heals you."—(Ex. 15-26)

To experience *The Unit's Moment in New Voice to the World,* go to Unity.org.

Beyond giving thanks, celebrating oneness with God, there are other types of prayers; petition prayers, asking God, once in the name of Jesus, your desire; pray for peace, prosperity, personal transformation, relationships, shared prayers, healing, faith being uplifted and affirmations. In the late 1800s, Myrtle Fillmore's life was transformed when she heard the idea, "I am a child of God, and therefore I do not inherit sickness". Speaking life-affirming words to her tuberculosis-riddled body, she went on to live a life of health and wholeness. News of Myrtle's prayer experience spread and people near and far began sending their prayer request to her.

In 1890, Myrtle and her husband, Charles Fillmore began a prayer ministry. That was 120 years ago. The prayers continue today. That was the beginning of Silent Unity. Do you have a prayer story to share? Everyone has a prayer story; be it for healing, prosperity, peace or personal transformation.

Marilyn Ferguson once said that we can allow disappointments, illness or injustices to clip our wings or to be the wind beneath them.

The choice is ours. We do not need to change the world; we only have to change our choices. St. Ignatius said, "Act as if everything depended on you; and trust as if everything depends on God."

Within the breast cancer experience, there is a difference between "healing and curing." As a breast cancer survivor, at first, I was very confused but learning the accepted definitions of healing and curing, I became better informed. Curing is "a remission or removal of symptoms that takes place in the body. It is the work of doctors and medicine." Healing is defined as the time and thought that it takes to reveal to ourselves the true nature of our lives; it is our wholeness. It takes place in the mind and the spirit of each individual in his/her own life." New faith is the substance of things hoped for." (Hebrew 11:1)

Prayers deepened my awareness of the healing power of God.

It quicken and renewed my body, mind and spirit as it made a positive difference in my live. Having breast cancer changed my world but did not take my life. "Rejoicing in our oneness with God and one another", breast cancer survivors celebrate healing in every aspect of our lives and in the world. "The Lord is my strength and my shield; in Him my heart trusts." (Psalm 28:7) There is an enemy who seeks to steal, kill and destroy (John 10:10) His name is Satan and he seeks to destroy us just as the hijackers destroyed the Twin Towers. The first line of defense is to be ready. Learning to deal with the live as a breast cancer took away the fear and lies that are associated with cancer. That's the power of prayers and faith.

Praying is a two way street. While prayer should be a two-way street, many spend far more time directing prayers to God, and far too little time listening to His directions. "He awakens me morning by morning, wakens my ear to listen like one being taught. (Isaiah 50:4)

Sharon Jaynes in her book *The Power of a Woman's Words describes how there is incredible power in your sphere of influence with the words you speak.* In allowing God to transform your heart, mind, will and emotions are new beginnings as well as fresh faith in God. Like God reminds us, "My grace is sufficient for you, for my power is made perfect in weakness" (2 Corinthians 12:9) Think about how you are one with God. Commit to seeing your blessings and make praying a way of life. "Delight yourself in the Lord and He will give you the desires of your heart". (Psalm 37:11)

The great 13th century mystic Meister Eckhart once said, "If the only prayer you can ever say in your entire life is "thank you," it will be enough. It is fitting to express gratitude Paul stated that God will supply all that you truly need. "Our God is able to do exceedingly abundantly above all that we ask or think, according to the power that works in us". (Ephesians 3:20)

The power of prayer brings wisdom, freedom, joy, prosperity and keeps you "plugged into the eternal source of spiritual power."

Be open to the ideas, inspirations, and resolve to live, sing and dance to the full spectrum of your spiritual growth. Create a sacred and powerful prayer consciousness and acknowledge the impact prayer has on your body, mind and soul. Prayer unites you in sacred communion with God and one another. Prayer consciousness spans the globe and your prayers are powerful. In Matthew 6:5 it reads:

"Whenever you pray, go into your room and shut the door and pray to your father who is in secret". Magdiel Martinez's thought for the day is "at the outset of any journey, seek divine wisdom." Prayers give you the grace and humility to deepen your relationship as well as friendship with Jesus.

Throughout your openness in prayer, you allow God's revelation to quickly unfold. Giving time to God, thru prayer helps to develop a prayer life. Open your Bible. Read Psalm 105. It might seem long but it has a simple theme: "Remember what God has done for you and thank Him. This should not be too difficult. John Ortberg, Jr. said "Prayer becomes real when we grasp the reality and goodness of God's constant presence with the real me". As you develop your spiritual maturity, you come to know that God is with you.

Seven

The Role of Prayer

In his book, *Coming Home To Your True Self,* *Albert Haase, O.F. M.* define prayers as a form of penance or as a spiritual discipline. Our prayers should make us more attentive to the presence of God.

The ongoing practice of developing a conversation with God is "deliberate practices" until the awareness fosters a prayerful, contemplative attitude becomes an expression of prayer without ceasing (see Luke 18:11; 1 Thessalonians 5:17)

Whatever form it takes, prayer makes for a heighten awareness of God's presence, in whom "we live and move and have our being" (Acts

17:28) When we pray, we become channels or instruments of God, making ourselves a "connecting point between heaven and earth to the Divine Power". Prayer align us with the "one power, presence and life". In *Science of the Mind, page 153,* "Whatever intelligence we have in this Spirit in us. Prayer is its own answer." Prayer, from the *Sermons of St. Anthony,* is directing our affections toward God. It is a devout and friendly talk with Him.

Prayer is thanksgiving. That is an acknowledgement of benefits received, and an "offering of all our understandings to God so that our prays may be a lasting one." Prayer makes us prayerful as it heightens our awareness of the presence of God, in whom "we live and move and have our being (Act 17:26) We become more aware of "Thee", not "me". As John the Baptist said of

Jesus, "He must increase, but I most decrease." (John 3:30)

Committing to a daily and seasonal practice of prayer should begin a spiritual journey that leads to spiritual wisdom and spiritual direction. This is hard work that demands time, discovery and motivation to discover God's grace and learn to be attentive to God's presence in your life. In this moment of transition, prayers aid in the discovery of God's presence and action in your life.

Entering into a prayerful conversation to discover, articulate and grow spiritually is a process, challenge and sometimes frustrating spiritual practice.

Prayers of any kind, whether it's with the Spirit or with the understanding, it is an absolute necessity if you want to be spiritually strong and ready in times of crisis. That's what Jesus urged Peter and the other disciples to do in the Garden of Gethsemane. He said, "Watch ye and pray, lest ye enter into temptation." The spirit is truly ready but the flesh is weak" (Mark14:38)

Instead of obeying Jesus's "admonition to pray", the Scriptures tells us that the disciples went to sleep. As long as you live, there will be temptations; therefore, it is necessary to "stay prayed up".

If you commit yourself to spend time each day praying, it will enable you to overcome weakness and build yourself up by praying. In Proverbs 20:27 it says, ". . . He gives light to your spirit so you know which way to go." Learn to communicate with God. Worship Him.

Sing to Him. Dance with Him. Listen to Him. Let God be the biggest thing in your life! "Practice the presence of God in your life". Pray!

Understanding put "feet" under your prayers and gives your spiritual a foundation to stand on. Don't work on developing understanding unless you are willing to change, ready to "be renewed in the spirit of your mind, and put on new nature, created after the likeness of God in true righteousness and holiness".

(Eph. 4:23-24) It is helpful to realize that the spiritual path is one of releasing and renewing. The "willingness" to center in knowing our oneness with the Spirit is the key to a continuous experience of spiritual growth and development. Today is the only day to declare change and transformation. This is the right moment. Direct the power of your prayers so that you are consciously and powerfully activating "the Law of Life to move in the direction of your higher good." Dr. Ernest Holmes reminds us of one of fundamental powers that we have as spiritual beings; the ability to start anew." Read often. Study diligently, Ponder it well and in your daily life put it into practice. Remember, in Psalm 119:105, "Your word is a lamp for my feet and a light to my path."

Tony Evans, senior pastor of the Oak Cliff Bible Fellowship in Dallas, Texas, stated *"when your spiritual energy is drained, He lead you to refreshment. When your life seems threatened outside your control, God promises His protection." Psalm 23 is more than just a lovely poem; it is a profound description of the relationship God offers you. No matter how things look, God is* constantly at work on your behalf and you can fully rely on His mercy and goodness.

Praying is a starting point. Each one is significant as well as Important. Praying does not necessarily remove the pain or difficulties. It provides comfort; gives a peace that can sustain you in the middle of any situation. The Bible says God has a surplus of grace; "And God is able to make all grace abound toward you, that you, always having all sufficiency in all things, may have an abundance of grace for every good work". (2 Corinthians 9:8)

Is it possible that God want you to be "selfish" in your prayers?

Even if you might think this, no, praying is not a "selfish" act but "supremely" spiritual request.

When we ask for God's blessings and or favor, we are crying out for the wonderful and unlimited goodness that only God has the power to give us." This kind of "richness" is what the writer was referring to in proverbs: "The Lord's blessings is our greatest wealth; all our works add nothing to it." (Proverb 10:22)

Let me tell you that prayers open your life to blessings, peace and miracles that only having a relationship with God can provide.

"Ask," promised Jesus, "and it will be given to you." (Matthew 7:7)

Through a simple, believing prayer, you can change your future.

You can change what happens in your life. If your purpose is to know Jesus, more than two millennia's ago, Jesus told His disciples how this can happen. He said, "Abide in me and I in you . . ." (John 15)

Ask God to enable you to spend your day as a co-worker with Him doing what He has "entrusted" you to do.

Prayer should make you more prayful. According to Albert Haase, "Whatever we do our time of prayer should have an effect on the way we live and act. Our prayers should make us attentive to the presence of God. This technique is a discipline. Ernest Holmes would say, through our affirmative prayer, God always says "Yes" to our little hops of faith. At some point Joel Goldsmith says to stop talking God and learn to experience him. Prayer's purpose is to know God, to awaken to and experience the Presence of the Spirit.

Roger Teel said that "genuine" spiritual development leads to wondrous spiritual joy; the security and joy of God in you.

Eight

Centered in faith

How do you develop faith in something you can't see?

How can you put your future in the hand of a power that is invisible?

The truth is that you do it every day. Electricity is invisible and you have complete faith when you flip the switch and your bill is paid the light will come on. Microwaves are invisible, yet when you place something in it to heat or cook that it will be heated and cooked.

In the twenty-first century, you are accustomed to having faith in invisible forces; radio, e-mail and cell phones are just a few.

Love is invisible. Joy is invisible. Peace is invisible. And yet you know that all three exist. Just because you cannot see it does not mean that it does not exist.

"If ye have faith as a grain of mustard seed, ye shall say unto the mountain, remove hence to a yonder place; and it shall remove; and nothing shall be impossible to you." (Matthew17:20) **The Science of Mind** teaches that God is always in your life. He is always present as the power that you need to make your dreams come true. Your reality is created by focusing your attention. Deepak Chopra stated "What you give attention to grows. If your attention is attracted to negative situations and emotions they will grow in your awareness."

Spiritual heath is "created by focusing your attention on all that is good and well in your life." Learn to focus your mind on all that is well.

Author Gary Zukav, in his book *Spiritual Partnership* describes how to be drawn to the right "Spiritual Partner" to assist to create, "authentic power . . . a life of meaning, fulfillment, gratitude, joy, creativity, and vitality." While finding and developing your spiritual partnership, be ever mindful that Jesus is the best friend you could ever have. He is your "BFF". Read John 15:9-17. Make a choice to concentrate your attention on things that most important in your life and the gratitude you feel for life.

In prayer, you become attuned to Divine wisdom and inspiration.

Jesus said, "He who follows me will not walk in darkness, but will have have the light of life" (John 8:12) Every day you have decisions to make; at home, on the job, in school or training programs. In each instance, you have access to divine wisdom and inspiration based on your faith. By using your faith, you can make a decision to work on your spiritually. A spiritual journey is like a "triathlon". Charles D. Kelsey stated, "To fully engage in a spiritual journey, we need balance in prayer, Bible study, and worship." These three activities will strengthen our spiritual lives so that we can accomplish what the writers of Hebrew calls "the race marked out for us." That is the race that leads to an experience of God that is based on faith.

Knowing that God does not guarantee a completely smooth ride, but with Him, you can endure "life's uneven road" is a great feeling.

The Psalm wrote, in Psalm 11:1, "In the Lord I take refuge." No matter how scary or uncomfortable the situation may seem, ". . . the Spirit of God does not make us timid, but gives us power . . ." (2 Timothy) 1:7 Throughout the Gospels, Jesus says "Fear Not".

Kristian Neff, wrote "Remembering you are not alone, take a deep healing breath and say these words to yourself:

May I be safe.

May I be peaceful.

May I be kind to myself.

May I accept myself as I am.

Your thoughts are powerful. Just as you can reset your computer when it malfunctions, you can reset your thoughts; shift your thoughts from fear and worry to hope and blessings in mind, body and spirit. Anytime is a good time to pray. Jesus did not limit prayer to a specific time, place and neither should you.

Remember that God is with always with you, and anytime is a good time to pray. "In all your ways acknowledge Him, and He shall direct your path". (Proverb 3:6)

How can you better yield to the Spirit's guiding in your own life?

Ask the Holy Spirit how you can broaden your vision to include new ways of spiritual growth. "For everyone that asketh, reciveth; and he that seeketh, findeth; and to him that knocketh, it shall be opened." (Luke 11:10) Remember that all things are possible through the power of God in you. You must not be discouraged if your growth seems slow. Make it enduring and peaceful by patience. When you experience growth, give God the glory as well as credit. There is a spirit in you that is greater than all the world.

Keep positive thoughts, words and action to create a healthy spirit.

Nine

Conscious Awareness

Andrew Harvey wrote that "Everyone who is destined to have a Spiritual transformation comes to the journey with a wound as big as God." In The **Science of Mind** it is written "Faith does not spring full-orbed into being, but grows by knowledge". There is value to be gained in every step of your spiritual journey. Take time for inner reflection and consultation with the Spirit. Allow the Spirit within you to reveal Its intent and purpose in your life.

Allow the Spirit to express through you in Its own way and time.

Trust in your inner guidance. Daily meditate on being receptive to what the Spirit wants to express in your life. Meditate on your intimate relationship with God and pray: "How beautiful is Your love . . . how much better is your love , , ," (Song of Song 4:10)

Meditate on Bible passages and live them until they become part of you. In Psalm 119:103, the Psalmist wrote: "How sweet are your words to my taste, sweeter than honey to my mouth."

Janice Ross said, "Through the Bible God speaks to us, nourishes us, and supports us. We are to read it regularly with faith, and follow its wisdom. When a passage from God's words gets our attention, it is not meant to be a cut-up word that we carry as a note stuck between the pages of our Bible."

By spending time with God's Word and in prayer, you become connected to God, the writer of Psalm 119 recognized the importance of a connection to God. By meditating on God's Word and then applying it, the psalmist stayed "connected" to God. The "spiritual pathway" is based on the ability to develop inner strength and connection to God. Let it sink in! You are a work in progress; moving forward to a greater spiritual person. Live, move and have your being in the "Intelligence of the Spirit."

Ram Dass wrote "the spiritual journey is individual, highly personal. It can't be organized or regulated. It isn't true that everyone should follow one path. Listen to your own truth." In order to pursue your own unique spiritual path, center into silence, turn within yourself and allow the "creative intelligence" within you to speak and reveal your true spiritually to you.

John E. Welshons in his book *When prayers Aren't Answered*, wrote "God protects us not by prohibiting anything bad from happening in our lives but by giving each and everyone one of us everything we need to handle anything that happens to us."

Author Joyce Meyers wrote "Only God can turn a mess into a message, a test into a testimony". To have a dance with God and celebrate what you share, especially the best part, His Love for you, is amazing. You owe it all to Him. Cross the dance floor, reach out and say thank you God. I've come full circle. "Let's look to the hill from which comes our help". (Psalm 121:1)

David Vantais said "It is not all about them; it is all about God.

Grow in awareness of God. Hebrew 4:12 states that "the word of God is living and powerful." Acknowledge that although we walk hand in hand, we also rest in the palm of "God's hand". Put aside your list of human wants and say these words: "God, I desire a closer walk with you. This is my only desire, for knowing you is enough."

Ten

Spiritual Techniques

Bishop T. D. Jakes said that he knows of no more powerful words than the Words of God. He stated that "the Scriptures are indeed living, powerful and sharper than any two-edged sword; able to touch and transform the deepest part of you." "Not that we are sufficient of ourselves" wrote Paul. To the end, he prayed that God would bless and strengthen them "with might through His Spirit."

(Ephesians 3:16) For the Father's touch, you ask every day.

Sue Silling in *Only Believe* wrote: "Spiritual life is not listening to the murmurings of the world but to that inner voice." Using powerful tools such as affirmations, prayers, meditation and daily practice. These techniques will help to address real life concerns. To assist you, you have been given a gift. Have you found your gift? If you have not found your gift, now is the time. You are on a mission.

Spiritual living is not easy but you are free to perform at your best.

You are emerging into the new self. Though you often speak as if you can plot your own course to live the life that you desire, it rarely happens. The emerging process is harder to follow then you would like to admit. Open yourself to God's guidance.

Allow prayers to keep you energized. One way to do that is to engage in meditation. Mary Alice and Richard Jafolla defines meditation as the conscious directions of one's attention to the inner self. They detail how one good meditative technique that works for most people is to simply observe your breathing. Simply become more aware of your breathing. As you do this, keep your breathing naturally. "In . . . and out. In . . . and out. In . . . out. Don't change the rhythm in any way. Concentrate on it. Actually experience it."

Another approach to developing spiritual growth is through affirmative prayers. Silent Unity defines affirmative prayer as a positive life-affirming approach to prayer. These prayers are used to reconnect with God and to focus on His infinite goodness. You can affirm prayers for yourself as well as others. Classic Unity prayers include: The Prayer of Faith, The Lord's Prayer, Prayer for Protection, Divine Order, Healing,

Prosperity, Travel, Protection, World Peace and World Leaders. For additional prayers, meditation and other spiritual resources, please visit www.silentunity.org. In Psalm 49-3, it is written: My mouth shall speak wisdom; "the meditation of my heart shall be understanding." You do not have to know how these work, only trust that it is working and that you are working with it. In due time, you will find yourself in a better place.

Embrace the new beginnings in your life. As Howard Thurman stated "Be sure to pray!"

As you realize how powerful your thoughts are, you begin anew with a new thought. After years of drug abuse, he no longer wanted to live. Johnny Cash described his spiritual experience as a rebirth.

He recalled, "I felt something very powerful start to happen to me, a sensation of utter peace, clarity, and sobriety." When you focus on God as your spiritual source, the "rest" falls into place.

Amazingly with an open mind, you can stretch to new dimensions and awareness. Allow your mind to be stretched in the light of God.

Practice spiritual discernment, as you become more aware of God.

Eleven

Zoom In

Remember that the most interesting subject you can study is yourself. Realizing this, the ancient Greeks placed over one of their temples the inscription, "Know thyself." There are many things that you might not know about yourself but you do know that God made you good. Keep this faithfully in mind and it will grow into expression in your life because it is the foundation of your existence.

Remember that you have inner spiritual strength that is capable of sustaining you when you need it. No matter how great your need may be.

There is no better way to progress on the spiritual journey than through prayer. There is no right or wrong way to pray, no rules or regulations, only the presence of God calling for your attention. You need only to make time for God, to commit to this purpose. Prayers can fill you spiritually. Learning "truth, gaining spiritual insight, and preparing for spiritual growth is a balanced combination."

"God is our refuge and our strength, a very present help in trouble" (-Psalm 46:1)

Turning to God in prayer is a conscious cooperation for God to guide your path. Spending time meditating as David is a start.

He said to the Lord, "I meditate on You in the night watches." (Psalm 63:6) and "I meditate on all Your Works; I muse on the works of Your Hands. I spread out my hands to You; my soul longs for you like a thirsty land" (143:5-6). And he prayed that the meditation of his heart would be acceptable in God's sight (Psalm 19:14) "Come to the Father . . ." words of a song that is used for praise dancing, a kind of imperative dance that is used in a lot of churches as a part of their services is called "dancing for the Lord".

The dance can be emotional as well as touching. Dancing before the Lord can be exhilarating. Watching the dancers, looking up toward heaven, spinning across the floor, gracefully stretching and reaching arms out toward the heavens as they praise the Lord in dance is most rewarding.

Rick Hamlin, from *10 Prayers You Can't Live Without*, says, "*To try to pray is to pray. You can't fail at it. It is the only human endeavor I can think of where trying is doing."*

Sometimes life rumbles you around. But God's presence can have the last say-so in your life. That is what God does. That's why the Bible says you're to be "looking unto Jesus, the author and finisher of our Faith" (Hebrew12:2).

I would like to say that by being a good Christian, you should know there are good days and bad days. God has the last word.

God has a plan and a purpose for your time and or season.

Proverbs 16:9 Says it best " A man's heart plans his way . . ."

He can meet you where you are and give you peace and joy. He is a perfect provider. Remember God promised that He would "supply your needs according to His riches in glory by Christ Jesus" (Philippians 4:19). Do not get needs and wants confused. God will only supply what you "truly" need. Remember too that you are to give thanks. Are you failing to remember who your provider is?

Like you, most of us have "to do" list which might include, grocery shopping, household chores and deadlines that often leave you exhausted. To keep from being overwhelmed, set aside morning hour and spend it with Jesus. Lay aside your agenda and allow him to guide you. As you prepare your spirit for the day ahead, Diane Graham said "come and enjoy the peaceful tranquility that only Jesus can give."

You know without a doubt that your Father loves you; not "maybe" or "perhaps", but *surely*. Dare to step out in Faith and live in trust that God supports you and supplies you with all that you need. Ernest Holmes wrote, "With God and company, business is always good." Who would dissolve such a Divines Partnership?

Everything required for your spiritual journey and growth is supported by God.

Through authentic exploration, praying, meditating and studying the Word you gain insight into how everything unfold under Divine order. Focus on the task at hand. Take slow, deep breath while chanting, "I am the Breath of God. I am breathing the Breath of God." Focus on the task with gratitude and move through it with ease. Pray, as Saint Prado Pio, "Lord, lead me each day to a closer relationship with you and help me to appreciate you. By your grace, Lord, I will accept the trials you are sending me, knowing that your comfort and strength will accompany them, so that they do not overwhelm me. Amen" Unity School of Christianity suggestions for Daily Meditation includes:

I am a child of the living God. The Spirit of God lives in me, guiding me and sustaining me.

- All things are possible with God who dwells within me. The blessings of God are being poured upon me in full measure.
- I am rejoicing continually in God's life, love and substance.

World Ministry of Prayers, united centers for spiritual living include the following personal affirmations:

- Gratitude

  I start this day in gratitude. I am grateful for this breath. I am grateful for all that I have. (. . . name them)

- Now

  Right here and now, God is. Since God is everywhere present, God is right where I am. In this now moment, all is well. I am here, fully present right now. Now is the appointed time. I am the light of God.

As you go about your activities, have a spring in your step.

Yesterday's disappointments have no power to cloud today.

Become still, listen and allow your thoughts and feelings to be Christ directed. "In the morning sow your seeds (Ecclesiastes 11:6)

The books that you read, the songs that you sing or listen to, the praise as well as inspirations are great influences to spur your-64-spiritual growth. Also, they teach you to rely on God's guiding presence. With faith, you transition and you are renewed.

Pray and recognize that you are a spiritual being. Dr. Norman Vincent Peale says "you can pray your way through any difficulty. If you are disheartened about anything, just pray and keep on praying".

Dr. Roger W. Teel says "genuine spiritual development activate avenues of joy and allow limitless source of God's power."

Joel Osteen puts it this way "you have not danced your last dance." If your dance defies the odds, still give God praise, He sees your efforts." God's looking at the fact that you are trying to dance. Program your feet. Stay in the game.

Keep God in first place. He will always have an "after this" plan for you. He will take the "scars and turn them into stars."

Look at the bigger picture. "Reflect, refocus", meditate and quietly affirm: Thank you, God! He is always with you, And anytime is a good time to pray. Through your thoughts and actions, begin a plan of spiritual renewal. Build on a solid foundation. Let go and surrender the outcome to God.

You have meaning and purpose because you are part of a spiritual outpouring that allows you to be free to express the real you. You are a unique individual and God is active in and through you. Guide your spiritual growth, pray, meditate and affirm that your life is good. In Thessalonians 5:17-18, it states" pray without ceasing, give thanks in all circumstances".

When your world is "rocked" by trails and evil events, you are urged to draw near to God. In Hebrew 10:22, it states hold fast to hope that you prosper. You can trust in the "author and and finisher" of your faith. (Hebrew 12:1-2) Focus on the strength and help you endure to grow in your faith. Your tomorrow will be determined by your faith in God. In the blank of an eye God can suddenly shift you from where you currently are, to where He desires you to be. God did not make a mistake. You are not finished. Remember your steps have already been ordered.

Twelve

Digging Deeper

"Arise, shine; for your light has come, and the glory of the Lord has risen upon you."

Isaiah 60:1

Do not lose sight of your goal, spiritual renewal. It is not easy to admit being flawed. Sometimes, you mistakenly think that your faith is primarily about understanding the truth of your faith or learning the Holy Scriptures. Your faith, at its core, is about your relationship with God and with Jesus. Ask for the grace to come to know Jesus more intimately. Take a moment to speak to God, to dance with Him as a friend speaks to a friend.

In the end, you are granted the tremendous blessings of knowing that you do very little at all by yourself. Again, it will all "balance" out if you get in touch with God's love as you draw into a closer real, living, growing relationship with Jesus.

"Digging deeper into your growth as followers of Jesus, reading the Bible is like a seed being planted in good soil. The seed planted in good soil represents those with an honest and good heart, who hears the word, apply it and with patience, produce a crop or fruit."

Read Luke 8: 4-15.

Strong faith, strong finish! Pray "Open my eyes that I may see wonderful things in your law" (Psalm 119:18 Make use of the tools. Study the Bible. Observe the text. Observe the Historical settings. And then ask the question. How does this apply? Maybe you should ask the personal questions. How do you relate what the author says to your personal life? What am I going to do with what I have learned? Pray about what you have learned. Pray for God's strength to help you grow through your study,

Remember the "Do-Nots"
* Do not read your own ideas into the scripture.
* Do not ignore the Bible's cultural, historical and literary applications.
* Do not br too literal (see Matthew 5:29, 30)

Just think! As God's child, no matter how hard your life might seem, Jesus will help you to grow deeper in faith. Ask the Holy Spirit to Transplant you as you broaden your vision to include new ways of growing spirituality. Pray that your seeds of faith, planted in love, grow into towering trees in God's kingdom. Thank God for the fellowship of believers He has planted in your life.

Perhaps growing spiritually means appreciating God's grace in deeper and deeper ways. Praise Him for his love. Pray Psalm145 aloud as a prayer of praise. Ask him to reveal to you how God's grace has affected you and how to depend on it in the future. Thank Him for loving you enough to guide you closer to Him. Pray that the Holy Spirit's cool breeze will refresh and encourage you to grow stronger in faith.

Thirteen

New Balance

"Balance" seems to be the self-help catchphrase these days. Life is long and has many phases. It will all "balance" out if you are attuned to what sustains your body and spirit. Close your eyes and imagine yourself in the presence of Jesus, dancing like the brook or the "dance of contemplation." For you are called to celebrate the mysteries of God 's patience and love. You must take the first step. Remember and be assured wherever you are, God is.

Read Scriptures to inspire you. To increase your Spiritual renewal

Includes but not limit God's Words. Make your own list. Below are are a few of my favorites Bible verses:

"I will never leave you nor forsake you".

-Hebrew 13:5

"If any of you lacks wisdom, let him ask of God"

-1 James 1:5

"If the Son makes you free, you shall be free indeed".

-John 8: 36

"He who is in you is greater than he who is in the world."

-1John 4:4

"Open my eyes, that I may see wondrous things from your law"

-Psalm 119:18

"This hope we have an anchor of soul, both sure and steadfast."

-Hebrews 6:1

"Put on tender mercies, kindness, humility, meekness longsuffering; but above all things put on love."

-Colossians 3:12-14

"We all . . . are being transformed . . . by the Spirit of the Lord."

-1 Corinthians 3:18

"The Lord is on my side: I will not fear."

-Psalm 118:6

"My strength is made perfect in weakness".

-2 Corinthians 12:9

"Imitate me, just as I also imitate Christ".

-1 Corinthians 11:1

"You have been my defense and refuge in the day of my trouble."

-Psalm 59:16

"If you know these things, you are blessed if you do them."

-John 13:17

"Turn to me with all your heart, with fasting, with weeping and with mourning."

-Joel 2:12

"He makes me lie down in green pasture; he leads me beside still water. He restores my soul."

-Twenty—Third Psalm

"Act as if everything depends on you; trust as if everything depended on God".

-Saint Ignatius

"Where your treasure is, there will your heart be also"

-Matthew 6:21

"If the Son makes you free, you shall be free indeed,"

-John 8:36

"Grow in the grace and knowledge of our Lord and Savior Jesus Christ"

-2 Peter 3:18

"You will be like a well-watered garden"

-Isaiah 38:11

Take another look at some other Bible verses. Make yourself available to the Spirit's leading. How can you better yield to the Spirit guiding in your life? God sees you. And as He watches your joyful dance, He smiles.

Think of a way to keep a continual steady balance as you meditate on the Bible promises or talking to Jesus based on your prayers.

Epilogue

"Show me the path I should walk, for I entrust my life to you."

Psalm 143-8

How do you grow and become strong in the Spirit? This is a question that you consider for self-evaluation? What will it take for you to grow and become stronger in the Spirit? Maybe this is a better question to address.

Ongoing conversation, prayer with scripture and communication with others or what today is called " practice of discernment" has its place, but so does prudence. Dig deeper! How can you "tune in" to how God is calling you? Spiritually connecting, in the end will lead you to where God wants you to be.

Daily praying, being honest with your own habits of thinking and acting are fundamental in approaching spiritual renewal. When you are rooted in a personal relationship with God, your spiritual choices will reflect God's will in your life. You can be assured that, as a child, of the most high He is ready to direct your life. You return God's embrace when you allow yourself to explore experiences of God's love in your life and extend this freedom and invitation to others.

In the First Letter of John, you read, "Beloved, we are God's children now; what we will be has not yet been revealed". What we do know is this: when he is revealed, we will be like him, for we will see him as he is" (1John 3:2)

Songs reach deep into our hearts and minds and today's psalms and themes of faith and trust are spectacularly featured in songs by Rich Mullins. Go to YouTube, and lookup Rich Mullins' "Step by Step". For three minutes you will hear him speak and then hear the Song. Listen to his music. Really pray with Psalm 63 and allow your soul to dance with God's words.

Discover how praying is a little like dancing . Like dancing, someone leads and some follows. As with dancing, a part of praying is learning to listen, learning to feel the rhythm. The change of season, interaction between earth, other times to make your own move and initiate a dance of your own choosing. There is no limit how you can choreograph into your spiritual life essential dances.

These dances may include· one of surprises, of growth and change, of response to the "heart's own season"; one in which all other part of the exuberant dance is toward oneness with God. There is no event too commonplace to offer in a joyous dance. For if it is not a dance of showmanship but a dance of allowing God to direct and redirect your efforts. It become a dance of "affective" prayers."

The tempo changes and you, too, undergo changes. A sort of spiritual "repotting", transition period provides what is needed and trust the "Gardener" of your soul to provide for your maximum growth and expansion. "Repotting" is the never-ending process of spiritual evolution, growth and renewal. There is no other way to accomplish most things in this world than by *just doing them.*

So is it with redefining your dear friend, God. It is a personal challenge. Remember only God opens channels through which God's blessings flow.

Open yourself and your spiritual life to divine revelation, gain deeper spiritual understanding and discover more for which you are thankful. God dances with you and blesses your expressions.

Dare to Dance!

Acknowledgments

When I think of the presence of God in my life, a strange excitement taps in my heart; one of growth, change and constant interaction with God. In this dance, thanks for leading me.

To my son, Regis Allison, Jr, wife Samantha and grand-children, thanks for a dance of sharing, love, imagery and surprises.

To my sister, Deborah Baker and family, my brother Preston Broussard, Jr. and family thanks for feelings and words that are like the brook dancing swiftly.

To my sister in Christ, Beatrice Schaffer, thanks for the dance of cooperation, dance of affective prayers and celebration. To my traveling angle, cousin Betty Joe Harris, thanks for the dance of understanding, love and constant interaction.

To my dear friends, Mary Ann and Carldell Cade, thanks for the dance of exploration and interaction.

To Lillian, Allen, Edna, Gen, Allen, Mae, Bach, Harold, thanks for the dance governed by prayer, listening, patience and resolution.

Notes

Notes

Notes

Notes